My Tears Didn't Change God's Mind

ROSE GREER

My Tears Didn't Change God's Mind

ROSE GREER

Forward By Reverend Christopher C. Herring

Published by River Walk Publishing LLC
San Antonio, Texas

DISCLAIMER: Please note the content of this book is taken from a personal journal that exhibits the emotional disposition of a broken heart. This manuscript is in no way an instrument to discredit anyone or any practice. Grammar in journal entries may reflect to some as incorrect as it is the nature of expression at the time of writing.

My Tears Didn't Change God's Mind

By

Rose Greer

Author Request can be emailed to: AuthorRoseGreer@gmail.com

Published by River Walk Publishing, LLC in the United States of America.

Christopher C. Herring, Publisher: cherring@aol.com

ISBN: 978-1-954787-16-2

HARD COVER ISBN: 978-1-954787-17-9

Library of Congress Number:

Acknowledgments

I would like to extend special acknowledgments to the following that have been a vital part in my conquering the deepest, darkest moments of my life. I humbly thank you!

Psychiatrist

Dr. Kanthi Raju

2150 Lakeside Blvd., Suite. 225

E. Richardson, TX 75082

Phone: 972-907-5230

Email: doc@drkanthiraju.com

Website: drkanthiraju.com

FAITH FAMILY

Bishop TD Jakes and The Potters House family

https://www.thepottershouse.org/

Reverend Christopher C. Herring

River Walk Publishing LLC

https://RiverWalkPublishing.com/

PSYCHIC MEDIUM

John Edward

https://johnedward.net/about/

Special Acknowledgment To My Husband Wade

Words cannot express the love and respect my heart holds for you. When we married 30 years ago, you became more than my husband. You embraced Troy Lee as YOUR son. You loved and taught him what it was to be a man and father without reservation, complaint or sweat.

In his transition, I've witnessed the depth of your love for him through your grief. Losing him seemingly left you lifeless because your love for him was beyond me, it was as if he had become a natural extension of yourself.

While I have focused seemingly solely on the depth of my grief and the need for your embrace and support, I recognize that your heart has been bleeding and screaming in silence too.

You are the epitome of a man that not only stepped up but was vulnerable enough to give your heart without restraint and to love beyond natural composition.

I am forever humble and grateful that you are my husband and the father of our children.

Loving You Forever,

Rose

Dedicated With an Everlasting Love

To all of those that have loved, supported, and held me together.
Even when I didn't know I needed it.

My children Tronicka, Victor (Son-in-Love), Cedric, LeeAnn and
Raymond (not blood but certainly a love child) who are my numberone
fans. Thank you for your encouragement, faith, and thoughtfulness.

My mom, Pastor Hazel Spain and her entire church familyfor their
kindness.

To my aunts Angela, Sandra, Juanita, and Alice for just dropping in to
check on me. To the little people that call me MiMi and make me smile,
I pray I never let you all down.

To the most wonderful sister circle a girl could ever ask for. Teresa,
Tammy, Sonya Denise (Neecee), Yolanda, and Vanessa. Thank you for
always being solid and so very thoughtful.

To my twin, Carl, for being honest even when the truth was painful for
me. For sharing the intimate details of the loss of his only child with me.
I am forever grateful to you. Even though you kept reminding me I
wasn't God.

To My Dear Friend and sister in parallel Rose Jacobs. I am honored that
in the distress of the transition of your daughter inNovember, of the
strength you exerted in the transition of my son in December. While grief
could have boxed you in, you reached beyond to be the support and
empathic companion needed during the unexpected. I am forever
grateful and honored that God spiritually connected us. May we continue
to live in the joy of the remembrance of our children.

My Tears Didn't Change God's Mind

Troy Lee is my firstborn son. He was a healthy, amazing 38-year-old that had just left his mom's house hours prior. He had such an amazing spirit. He was affectionate. He loved hugs and kisses. My biggest cheerleader. If no one else thought my idea was great, Troy did. Our relationship was so closely knitted that the thought of me never being able to see him or speak to him again was non-existent. He was an extension of me. If I was, he was, and that's how it was supposed to be.

I will never forget the phone call that changed my life forever. 4 am Christmas morning, 2018. My daughter called and said they were rushing him to the hospital. My immediate response was, what could have happened? I rushed over to the hospital. He had been in crisis before, he may have come out with a few scratches or scars, but he came out. Something was wrong, but I was confident he would be okay. I know God was always with us, and He would meet me at the ER. What I didn't realize was, what I thought I knew, I really didn't. This trip to the hospital would be the last time I would see my son alive.

When I heard the sound of the machine flatline as I held his hand, my son's spirit spoke to my spirit, and I knew it was time. My precious, perfect son was leaving me. I had just seen him not even 24 hours before in what I thought was perfect health, and I was now watching him take his last breath.

I couldn't save him. I wanted to, but I couldn't. I wanted to trade places with him, but I couldn't. Where was God? Why didn't He come to our rescue as many times before? He has the power of life and death. Is He asleep? Is He on vacation? My heart had been stolen, and God let this happen.

Troy Lee was transitioning, and I could not stop it. I'm his mom, and I was supposed to be able to fix this. I was overwhelmed with emotion and despair. I felt helpless, hopeless, broken, bewildered, abandoned, betrayed, and forsaken . . . How do you recover when a hole is left in your soul? Only if you were here with us, Troy Lee. Without you, our lives would never be the same.

Author's Intent

In sharing some of the most intimate details of my journey after the loss of my son, my goal is to be honest and transparent. I only wish that someone was honest with me before this experience about their pain. Honest about their disappointment in God and in themselves. Maybe, just maybe, it would have saved me from myself. Saved me from my anguish.

I want you to be clear. Loss is loss. Whether you've lost a child by death, a miscarriage, a close relationship/friendship, parent, spouse, business, or even yourself. Whatever you have lost or will lose that is dear or relevant to you is loss, and no one can take that seat for you. I've learned many may want to be you, but no one will ever want to pay the price it costs to sit in your seat.

Loss is a process, and the best way to heal is through truth. It's important we as human beings understand it's okay not to be okay. I pray that my honesty and transparency will help you to take your voice back. I pray that my emotional roller coaster ride of undiluted reality will cause you to breathe again. It is my desire in love that my experience in written expression will reach the hurtful, painful, shameful, grieving places in your heart and spirit and provoke healing.

Thank you in advance for journeying with me through my truth, embracing healing for you and for me.

With My Best Regard,

Rose

Forward

When your life is turned upside down and emptiness fills previously occupied spaces of joy and happiness, we seek a desperate response to understand why. We get consoled from family, from the world and even from God. Life can prove itself to be very hard as the person may not understand what just happened and how they really feel.

When Rose answered the phone at 4AM on December 25th, 2018… her whole world scattered before her eyes. Her tears fell to the floor and she felt God didn't answer her call to stop the pain.

When the phone rings, and the voice on the other side delivers news that is not good news, we struggle in our flesh, and our spirit is crushed.

To understand how I was to respond to Rose, I turned to my Bible, and read the book of Job, to try to understand what does a parent feel like after losing their child. What should her response be? In his story, Job, and his wife lost 10 children all at once. As we are trained in Sunday School, we looked at the tragedy from Job's perspective – as he is the main actor. Job was credited for loving and honoring God despite losing everything including his children.

On the other hand, reading the text closer, Job's wife reacted much differently. She said to her husband to "Curse God and die". This unnamed woman, wife, and mother became a villain in many sermons simply because of her emotional response that said to her husband "Curse God and die". Rose's first book under this topic was "Damn, God" with the subtitle **My Tears Didn't Change God's Mind.** It was received harshly by the community – probably because it resembled cursing God, and probably because Christian people have developed an ear to hear and see things only from the very best of what they have learned in the faith. I understand because in my counsel to Rose, I too judged. But after reading Job and even the fall of Eve in Genesis, where she lost her first-born children, the agony these mothers experienced and their grieving and pain, God did hear them. For my friend Rose, God did hear. He asked me to ask her to change the title to the subtitle. She accepted the offer.

Today as she preaches, and Sisters call her Minister, or Lady Rose, or

Lady Greer, these are titles she never saw coming before her son passed away. But God had his plan for her life…and she's just beginning!

Today, as I reflect on her book, and remember working with mothers, grandmothers and aunts who lost a child due to senseless violent deaths, or police shootings, or suicide, it became apparent that I saw this same spirit of loss that mothers tend to show more fiercely than fathers. I was told mothers nurture differently and more loving and so their connection is much stronger! This curse God spirit is what Rose is completely transparent and has left nothing to the imagination. Her hope is the Spirit dies and you find life within your pain.

As individuals maybe, we are to think and recognize how different men and women think about issues like death. Maybe we should spend time to learn how to show more compassion and not to villainize a mother who is in pain because of the loss of her child. Maybe we need to get out of the corner of judging but spend more time in our Word and closet of prayer. Let us agree to let God sort out the mysteries that we may never understand.

From the ministry position, when we hear a sister or brother who has experienced the worst news ever, let's develop a neutral call to action. What I mean is JUST LISTEN. Even as they are left standing empty or cursing God, Listen and pray on there behalf later. It is not necessary for you to defend God, but to pray that God heal the hearts and bring his understanding. Let the Holy Spirt convict us as He knows us.

Again, I speak from what I have witnessed. Like Rose, the person grieving is more than likely to retreat to lay down and to get off their feet. The words that come out of our mouths are heard to them as garble, gibberish as they are mourning. Their truth is no longer truth and the light becomes darkness. Only time with their Creator will cause something to happen. Please prepare yourself for a marathon in their healing and not a fast race.

Sometimes the best we can do is listen and listen and listen. Do not accuse your friend, or family member in their moment as we saw in Job. Just listen as they shed their tears and start the healing process.

Suffering the devasting loss of a child can lead to parents feeling lost and alone in their grief. We share with them to "put their faith and trust in God and know that He will never abandon you" is what we say.

How we respond to death, disease or misfortune that strikes the core of life, defines our true character. Rose' story is no different than Job and his unnamed wife for she lost her "perfect son" to death.

Later, after time and revelation from God Himself, what Rose' character revealed was a response to minister. This calling is much different than what she ever thought she was called to do as a businesswoman. God is ordering her steps to help the world see Him from a different perspective.

When Mothers lose their children before they reach old age, and these girls and boys are the apple of their eyes, know that God is still on the throne. Our hope is that as you encounter Eve's, the nameless wife of Job, and even our modern-day Rose, minister to their hearts but don't condemn them with your judgement. They may cuss and scream, but God can handle it more than you ever will know. He created them.

I am so proud of my friend who bravely took up the cross, and even drank from the cup of bitterness, to be on this path of healing and forgiving. Rose is leading souls to Christ through her family tragedy. Well done Rose, continue to preach the gospel and console the brokenhearted...

In Christ,

Reverend Christopher C. Herring
ChristopherCHerring.com
Publisher, River Walk Publishing, LLC

Table of Contents

SPECIAL
TRIBUTE

In my experience, I have identified a class of women that society has forgotten about. No one speaks on behalf of a mother who has never had the opportunity to hold her baby. While miscarriages, sudden instant death syndrome (SIDS), Still borns and abortions happen every day, the pain, emptiness, and anguish of that loss are so often overlooked. There is a feeling of shame that a mother has to endure for not coming home with her baby. Embarrassment for having an empty car seat.

Love doesn't begin at the first sight of the baby after delivery. Love begins at the realization of conception. The expectancy, the joys, the fears, the goals, the planning, and preparation is all a part of the process to welcome that new extension of you into the world. Many don't consider the pain of a mother who went into a hospital with a diaper bag full of tiny little diapers, the specially picked going home outfit, the baby lotion that you can't wait to smell, the car seat in place, the nursery fully decorated with the perfect theme to bring your baby home to, only to leave the hospital with no baby.

That mother has shared the growth of her baby inside of her. She's already begun to identify their personality by their movement. She's already experienced their responses to certain movements and emotions that she may have. She has become one with his or her heartbeat and can't wait to meet them face to face. Can you imagine all the people waiting to see the baby? All those that witnessed the pregnancy, helped with the planning, sent gifts, and who all awaited the arrival. Then sadly, this expectant mother has to come home empty-handed. This, too, is a major loss.

What that mother would give for late nights, teething, first steps, first words, diaper rashes, and colic. She has a void that no one sees, a pain no one feels, a shame no one understands, and a scream no one hears. She, too, feels broken, betrayed, robbed, empty, and like a failure. She, too, questions, *where did I go wrong, what could I have done differently, is God punishing me?* Even if this mother has other children, she still grieves the one because it still is an extension of her that she carries in her heart eternally.

You can never minimize someone's loss; too it will get better. You can always try again or look at what you still have left. The reason being, you may not see it, but she will always long for the part of her that's lost.

I want to speak to and on behalf of those and say I feel your pain. I understand your emptiness and the depth of your loss. On behalf of anyone, that has ever written off your pain as unimportant or insignificant, I humbly say I apologize. You are entitled to your tears, and your grief is real. When you can't find the words and can't share your pain because no one understands, I want you to be clear that your loss matters and your memories are real. The missing link is still yet a part of your everyday life, and no one can take that away from you.

I was selfish to think that having 38 years, 2 months, and 21 days were not enough with my son when realizing that someone never had the chance to hold their baby. Someone only had a minute, hours, maybe a few days, weeks, or months with their child. Now I realize I was very fortunate and blessed for the time I did have. I'm even more humbled that the pain from the loss of my son has heightened my vision to allow me to see the pain of those whose loss was far more premature than my own.

In memory of my loving niece Keanna (Yanna) Young and her stillborn son, Cannon. I finally understand.

CHAPTER

1

THE VOICE BEHIND
THE WORDS

To know me is to know that I am a perfectionist. Presentation means everything to me. People's perception of me mattered. My goal every day was to ensure that I gave people the right impression about Rose Greer in business, family, work, and in ministry. When people saw me, their impression of me was that Rose had it together. She was successful, had good kids, and a perfect life. I like to consider myself favored by God. I know He loves me, PERIOD. God has always been there for me, and He has always heard me and answered.

There was nothing wrong with my faith or my focus. I was a happy, bubbly social butterfly all the time. I never saw disarray. I was prim and proper; everything had to be right because I felt like it mattered.

This boisterous confidence was the nature of who Rose Greer Author was before my experience. After the loss of my son, I had to face the reality I'm not perfect. The pretense was over. I was a portrait of a mess. GOD HAD REMOVED MY COVERING. I thought I would walk in favor of the Most High until I took my last breath. Things like this don't happen to my family and me. We were immune from these sorts of devastations, so I thought.

I realized I possessed a false sense of security and knowing. I had lost my son, my marriage on life support, almost lost my business, almost bankrupt, and my other kids were trying to manage their grief while looking at their superhero example of a mom reduced to broken pieces. In my humanness, I longed for death. I now knew what Job felt like. God allowed the enemy in my camp and caused me to experience reality. Brushing my teeth, washing my face, and taking a bath were no longer important to me. My will and my mind no longer functioned at the normal capacity. My normal had now become abnormal, and my life would never ever be the same.

This loss has re-defined me, and now I see life circumstances and situations from an entirely new perspective. I, Rose Greer, am changed forever.

2

CAPACITY OVERLOAD

No one understood the pain. Friends and family who wished me the best only made things worse by trying to say the right things. They couldn't know how broken I was or how hurtful it was to hear their casual reassurances. And I couldn't tell them why. Couldn't play along, couldn't dress things up, couldn't tell them what I was going through as long as he wasn't there to hear it, too.

I couldn't eat, and though I dragged myself through the days, I couldn't sleep at night, either. I was barely functional, a stove with a cold pilot light. People used to turn to me for help. Now I couldn't even save myself.

Every attempt to reassure me felt like a mockery. I was lost and in constant agony, and no one seemed interested in knowing what I was enduring or why. They expected me to bounce back, to put my grief in its place. They didn't know how impossible that was at the time, and they didn't care to know. Their little speeches and snippets of scripture, the cliches they'd picked out of the air, just made me feel more alone.

And more bitter. I was alone, abandoned even by God. If God was silent, anyone who spoke was just flapping their gums. *Insultingly so*, I thought. When I couldn't hold my tongue, I lashed out, damaging some of my most meaningful relationships and destroying some.

Worst of all was being reminded that I was a "strong black woman." What on earth did strength have to do with anything? Was it a sign of strength that I was forced to endure this agony alone? To withhold my grief just to make others more comfortable? I was broken. I spent entire days desperately gasping for air and feeling the undertow threaten to take me back down under the waves.

Each time someone mentioned my loss, I relived my son's last moments. Their words would fade into distant whispers while I stayed in that excruciating point in time when he departed forever.

I am not a pack animal for pain. Nothing about me is strong enough to endure this, especially on anyone else's terms. Not my gender, not my skin tone, not my ancestry, not my past. Nothing you know about me prepared me for this ordeal. Nothing makes my pain less relevant. I am not strong enough for this. Grief is how we respond to the unbearable, and I am grieving. Praise my strength, and you spit in my face.

Every loss hurts. Some losses are fundamentally different from others. The loss of a child isn't just more intense than the loss of a parent or a friend: it is a different and more ferocious beast altogether. You devoted every bit of hope for the future to your child's upbringing. The world is an imperfect place, and you're an imperfect person, but you loved your child perfectly. That may have been the one constant in their lives, but it should have been enough. Your love was a thread connecting you to the best of your ancestral past and your deepest and most earnest hopes for a future you would not live to see.

When that thread was cut, all of the love and hope that it carried was cut, too. The love and hope that put life in your limbs each morning, that kept you from ever truly wondering if your hard work and sacrifice were worth it, gone forever.

No other kind of loss can serve as a model for the loss of a child. Not the loss of a close friend, or a beloved parent, however much those may have hurt. That doesn't stop people from drawing on the griefs they have known and trying to offer their help.

Every time someone told me that everything would be all right, I felt like cussing them out. He's gone. That's not all right. It never will be. Every time someone reminded me that at least I had other kids, it felt like they were damning us all. I'm not the only one grieving here. None of us is all right. And how dare you speak of my family the way you'd describe a box of donuts after one fell on the floor.

The only way past the grief is through the grief. Very few people around me understood that.

The truth of the matter is you're damned if you do and damned if you don't. Damn!!! God.

CHAPTER

3

GOD WHERE
ARE YOU?

Who can feel my pain?

Who knows the depth of my emptiness?

Brokenness and sorrow have become my portion. There is a huge, dark, black, empty hole in my soul. I can literally feel the empty place in my chest that was stolen from me. It feels sunk in, just empty. Nothing matters. I was angry, and I could not hear. I couldn't hear people, and I couldn't hear God. The phone ringing, the doorbell dinging; I couldn't hear it. The silence was consuming, and there were no words, just pain. My thoughts were no longer thoughts, just silence. Communication can no longer exist because of the weight and depth of the pain. I now understand the little girl's silence from the book "I Know Why The Caged Bird Sings". Her trauma caused her to be silent.

I feel like a vessel with a bunch of holes in it that no longer has the capacity to hold anything. It's like my favorite glass in the whole world slipped out of my hand and shattered into little pieces. That glass will never be able to hold water again. I tried hard to put the pieces back together, but it's impossible, and this was unbelievable.

I asked God, was He freaking asleep?
Yes, me and my saved, sanctified, filled with the Holy Ghost self questioned God. He could have saved my son, but He didn't. There are so many evil people in the world, yet you chose to take my precious son. I'm bitter, broken, angry, and mad as hell!
What is happening?
Why is this happening?
Does God not like me anymore?
Does He hate me?
What did I do?
God, can I make it right?
Can I fix this?
Do you need my help to bring Him back?
What do you want from me? Oh my God, the anguish, the pain, the unanswered questions.

GOD, WHY AREN'T YOU ANSWERING ME?

Religious people say you shouldn't question God. Well, you know what? I'm done with religion.

I tried so hard to leave God. How can I still love God when He took my son?
How can I still trust God after He betrayed me?
No one ever knows this feeling until they are there. I had questions, and who better to ask than the one responsible? I remember being in the closet on the floor in the fetal position crying out to the same God I hated to

help me. I needed answers, healing, resurrection, something. The thing was, I was so consumed with my grief that if He did reply, I still couldn't hear. Mixed emotions, thoughts of suicide, feelings of abandonment and betrayal, how do I live beyond this?

Is God trying to take me out?

He could have done that in the beginning and I wouldn't be experiencing this death in the flesh.

God, can you hear me?

Where are you?

And please tell me WHYYYY?

To answer the questions of man, I wasn't questioning God; I was questioning what He was doing. I didn't lose my faith; I lost religion. Now I have transitioned from religion to relationship.

CHAPTER

4

JOURNEY
WITH ME

At the onset of writing this book, I was just able to say my son has transitioned. I couldn't talk to others, and I couldn't speak to Troy. I was angry with God, and most days, I didn't think He was listening. These journal entries are a reflection of my inner pain and rollercoaster of emotions. I experienced a plethora of mental, emotional, and spiritual dispositions; from disbelief to anger and bitterness, betrayal and bargaining to reflection and acceptance.

This journey isn't easy. It doesn't happen overnight. I was entitled to every emotion that I wrote and lived. I had a lot of things going on inside of me that my mouth could not utter. As a result, these are the conversations I could never have. No one really understands, but as I write, my pain speaks.

I encourage you, if there is any ounce of pain in you, any ounce of grief, regret, embarrassment, disappointment, fear, anger, whatever the emotion may be, as you read my written expressions, you too can grab the pen and release what's bottled up inside. There's more room out than in. I learned that what I couldn't say with my mouth, I could say it with the pen.

I CAN'T BELIEVE THIS IS REAL

1/18/2019

I found someone who can communicate with my son. I'm desperate. I haven't left the house this month. I've called pastors to give me a word. That wasn't what I was looking for. I found a Medium, Clayton Rouge. He came to the house today. He defined you in detail. He said things you would say to confirm your presence was with him. He spoke distinctively about other family members you met and delivered messages that I was not necessarily looking for, but it was making the experience real for me. I began to cry uncontrollably because he didn't say you were pulling a prank on me. I really wanted this to be a lie that you weren't coming back.

_____

_____

_____

_____

_____

_____

_____

_____

_____

_____

_____

_____

_____

_____

_____

_____

_____

_____

HOW AM I SUPPOSED TO BE WITHOUT YOU?

1/20/2019

I'm missing my son. I finally realized today that I'll never see him physically anymore. Troy Lee, I'm still in love with you, just like I was the day I heard your heartbeat. We managed to grow up together, and we both turned out pretty good. It's amazing to me that the time we had wasn't enough. My soul aches for you, and my heart has a big hole in it now. I know now that this pain is the measure of my love. I keep trying to bargain with God, and it changes nothing. If you were here, we would work through this together. How am I supposed to be without you? Today is your little brother Cedric's birthday, and I forgot. I didn't even tell him Happy Birthday. And to think Cedric never even mentioned it.

_____

_____

_____

_____

_____

_____

_____

_____

_____

_____

_____

_____

_____

_____

_____

_____

_____

_____

_____

_____

_____

I'M LIVING A NIGHTMARE.

1/21/2019

My reminder to myself: There are no accidents with God, nor is He surprised by anything. God uses even the most horrendous circumstances for our good. Every circumstance comes to us for a purpose, bound by God's love and His plan and faithfully delivered with His permission. While we cannot go back and change the events, we can change the way we respond to the hurt it caused and decide how much power we are going to give to it today. I'm living a nightmare.

My Tears Didn't Change God's Mind!

_____

_____

_____

_____

_____

_____

_____

_____

_____

_____

_____

_____

_____

_____

_____

_____

_____

_____

WE MAY NOT ALWAYS UNDERSTAND OR EVEN LIKE HIS PROCESS, BUT WE CAN ALWAYS TRUST HIS HEART OF LOVE FOR YOU!

1/22/2019

Only God can take the broken pieces of your life and make something beautiful out of each one. He is waiting for you to let go of your pain and trust Him. No one loves you like He does. We may not always understand or even like His process, but we can always trust His heart of love for you!

Later that day . . .

As I sit here on the bed, in all black, I realize my earlier entry was me being the pastor's daughter because I don't believe what I wrote. As a minister myself, I was trying to preach or convince myself that God has to love me, but I didn't believe it. I was trying to convince myself that God was faithful and something good was supposed to come out of this, but I really didn't believe it. I was trying to play the part, but it wasn't real. I was trying to justify this pain God was allowing, but nothing I said convinced me that God was who I had believed or knew Him to be all of my life.

_____

_____

_____

_____

_____

_____

_____

_____

_____

_____

_____

_____

_____

_____

_____

_____

_____

_____

_____

_____

_____

_____

I CAN'T LET YOU GO; I'M SURE I NEVER WILL.

1/23/2019

To my son, I'm having a hard time accepting the fact that I'll never see your handsome face, the cleft in your chin, your coy smile, and the gleam in your eyes. I can't breathe, and my heart is racing. The pain hasn't let up any, and I don't think I'll ever know joy again. Not only were you my son, but you were also my first love, my reason to be the best. Now you're gone from the natural world and took a huge piece of me with you. I can't let you go; I'm sure I never will. Lee got sick today, and I lost it. All I could think was not again God. But she was okay. Thank you for watching over us.

My Tears Didn't Change God's Mind!

_____

_____

_____

_____

_____

_____

_____

_____

_____

_____

_____

_____

_____

_____

_____

_____

_____

_____

_____

_____

_____

THEY SAY TIME HEALS ALL WOUNDS. THEY LIED.

1/24/2019

Hey Troy Lee, this day has not been pretty. I've cried at leasta thousand tears today, wondering where you are and when will this nightmare end. This can't be real because I'm a goodperson, and you're amazing, and stuff like this doesn't happento us. We treat people kindly, we operate with integrity, we help others freely, not expecting anything in return. We love and care for others freely. So why am I in this club that I never agreed to enter (parent of a deceased child club).

Whose idea was this anyhow? I know there are people that probably deserve to leave this natural life: murderers child molesters, racists, rapists, sex traffickers, and the list goes on and on. This hurts, hurts like HELL!!! I can't pray, I can't meditate, and you know all the good advice I give; I don't have one word for myself.

They say time heals all wounds. They lied. I miss you more today than yesterday. They said the hurt of losing someone isequal to the love you had for that person. I love you so mucha piece of me left, my soul aches, and there is a hole where my heart used to be. I know our love story will never ever end, but I wish you were here with me. Mommy loves you, Troy Lee.

I KEEP TELLING HIM I'M STILL WAITING ON YOU TO STOP BY

1/25/2019

Why do people keep putting unrealistic expectations on me by giving me a healing deadline date? People act like they don't recall when David became King, the people mourned Saul. Even though God said he had given them a man after his own heart. The people mourned, and he was just King. Troy Lee is the flesh of my flesh. Troy Lee keeps reminding me that he might not walk through the door, but he's still in the room with me. I keep telling him I'm still waiting on you to stopby, drink a bottle of coke and eat any leftovers you can find.

My Tears Didn't Change God's Mind!

_____

_____

_____

_____

_____

_____

_____

_____

_____

_____

_____

_____

_____

_____

_____

_____

_____

I MISS YOU . . . I MISS YOU . . .

1/31/2019

Troy Lee I miss you so much I never thought in a million years that I would have to go a day without you. I never thought in a million years I'd have to go a day without hearing your voice or without seeing you. It just dawned on me. I hope you know just how much I love you and how much I want you to know how you make me a better person.

I miss you . . . I miss you . . .

I jumped out of the boat and realized I couldn't walk on water.

_____

_____

_____

_____

_____

_____

_____

_____

_____

_____

_____

_____

_____

_____

_____

_____

_____

_____

Rose Greer

I STILL CAN'T BELIEVE IT.

2/1/2019

Another day without my son being here in the physical world. I still can't believe it. My heart still aches, and my mind won't accept this. I've found myself angry, hurt, lost, and confused.

CAN SOMEONE PLEASE TELL ME HOW?

2/2/2019

I woke up crying and screaming because my son wasn't here. Crying out to God for understanding. Declaring that this has to be a mistake. Children aren't supposed to transition before their parents. That's not what I planned, not what I ever imagined, and I'm expected to just keep going, keep breathing, keep putting one foot in front of the other. Can someone please tell me how?

IT'S THE LITTLE THINGS THAT I MISS.

2/3/2019

I can't let go. My soul cries to see my son; hear him call out to me; have him make me laugh until my side aches. I just wantto hear him tell me to look like a real granny. It's the little things that I miss. This hurt is not easing up. My heart isn't less broken than it was a month ago. God help me, please if you don't help me, the sorrow will kill me. I have to ask the same God that allowed my son to be taken from me to ease my pain, the same God that I'm angry with, the same God that didn't breathe life back into his body.

I NEED YOUR HELP LIKE I'VE ALWAYS NEEDED YOU.

2/5/2019

Today I thought I heard your truck. Today I still don't understand, and I picked up my phone to call you. Troni had to remind me that you're no longer able to answer me. I need your help like I've always needed you.

_____

_____

_____

_____

_____

_____

_____

_____

_____

_____

_____

_____

_____

_____

_____

_____

_____

ALL THINGS ARE TEMPORARY EXCEPT LOVE; IT LASTS FOREVER.

2/6/2019

I'd give my life just to see you walk through the door once more. My first love, Troy Lee Webb. I miss you every second of every day.

LeeAnn reminded us All things are temporary except Love;it lasts forever. An amazing son, brother, father, and friend.

My Tears Didn't Change God's Mind!

_____

_____

_____

_____

_____

_____

_____

_____

_____

_____

_____

_____

_____

_____

_____

_____

_____

_____

I WISH . . . I WISH . . . I WISH

3/20/2019

I just realized yesterday that he's not going to call again. My call log has decreased substantially, and so has my message notifications. I wish I had answered every call now. I wish I could've stopped him from ever growing up. I wish I could go back to the first time he ever got into trouble, and PawPaw Kennard helped me fix it. (He had a surrogate pawpaw that was in law enforcement and a superhero mom. Yes, he was spoiled). I wish I could spoil him some more and hear him proudly say, "Yes I'm a Momma's boy so Now What!"

I wish . . . I wish . . . I wish

_____
_____
_____
_____
_____
_____
_____
_____
_____
_____
_____
_____
_____
_____
_____
_____
_____
_____
_____
_____

PTSD

4/3/2019

I know for sure this pain will never end because my love will never die. Here I go again with another anxiety attack. I can't breathe, my fingers are tingling, so are my toes, my heart is racing, and my chest hurts like hell. And everybody wonders why and how I can be angry with God. My son was gone in an instant, and I'll never be the person I once was. Yesterday the new physician said she believes I'm suffering from Post-Traumatic Stress Syndrome, better known as PTSD, from the sudden trauma of losing my son. I don't know if she's right or not, but at least there's a name for what I'm suffering through. She also was honest enough to say no one knows why we were chosen for this journey.

How can I not be angry at the God who is good, kind, merciful, and all-knowing? He knew that this would destroy me; He knew the pain it would cause. Who else is to blame? I can't seem to find hope, just pain.

In pain, there is always hope for those who are courageous enough to just find joy no matter what stage you find yourself in.

_____

_____

_____

_____

_____

_____

_____

_____

_____

_____

_____

_____

_____

_____

_____

_____

_____

_____

_____

POWERLESS

4/4/2019

My mind is all over the place. I'm pissed because I'm not the woman I was the day before I lost my son. I'm angry becauseI now suffer in silence behind a fake a** smile. I'm powerless,and I don't like it.

My emotions change from minute to minute.

As the days go by, I'm learning all about powerlessness, and I don't like this lesson. I've realized the secret is to not be afraidof it— not to run away.

If I'm honest, I AM scared.

I'm scared of my children leaving me because I don't have answers or wisdom for them right now—because I'm not useful to them right now.

I'm scared of what I'll look like if I don't shake the grief . . . I'm scared of what I'll BE like . . . on the other side of this transition.

I'm afraid of my own mortality.

I'm afraid of dying without fulfilling my destiny.

ALL of these fears have one thing in common: I am powerless against them.

There's nothing I can DO about any of them.

But there is a silence in acceptance.

And that's where I am right now.

I wish I could surrender.

Today, everything changes. I hope.

I'M EMOTIONALLY AND SPIRITUALLY BROKEN. PHYSICALLY WEAK WITH NO REAL RELIEF IN SIGHT.

4/5/2019

The fact that I have been grieving the loss of my son, the possible end of my marriage, along with trying to salvage my business. Now a diagnosis of PTSD, panic attacks, and anxiety and feeling like I have lost it all.

I'm lost, angry, scared, and worried because I can't produce, and I don't want to anymore. EVERYTHING I love seems tobe under attack. I'm emotionally and spiritually broken. Physically weak with no real relief in sight.

God isn't speaking during my test. He's silent, and I don't or can't understand. The death of everything I knew to be true has shaken my faith, but something in my spirit is telling me to trust the process. To step into my faith, to hold on to His hand to yield myself completely.

HOME

4/7/2019
I Heard Your Voice In The Wind Today — Unknown
I heard your voice in the wind today
and I turned to see your face;
The warmth of the wind caressed me
as I stood silently in place.

I felt your touch in the sun today
as its warmth filled the sky;
I closed my eyes for your embrace
and my spirit soared high.

I saw your eyes in the window pane
as I watched the falling rain;
It seemed as each raindrop fell
it quietly said your name.

I held you close in my heart today
it made me feel complete;
You may have died... but you are not gone
you will always be a part of me.

As long as the sun shines...
the wind blows...
the rain falls...
You will live on inside of me forever
for that is all my heart knows.

THE PAIN OF YOU LEAVING IS CONSTANT WITH NO RELIEF IN SIGHT.

4/8/2019

Where did you go? Why did you leave? I wasn't ready to say goodbye. My heart longs to hear you, my arms want to hug you, and my eyes want to see that smile. Every day my heart breaks over and over because you're not here. My eyes stop crying every now and then, but my soul screams in agony, and the tears won't retreat. The pain of you leaving is constant with no relief in sight. I scream for God to help me, but then I'm reminded that He took you away, and I'm angry all over again.

I'M HELPLESS AT THIS MOMENT, FROZEN WITH GUILT AND A MILLION QUESTIONS.

7/17/2019

I'm standing still dealing with the pain of losing my firstborn, my champion, my hero, my confidant and my friend. Wanting to move, but I can't breathe. So as my mind wanders and I drift between anger and hurt. I finally remember there's Tronicka, my beautiful daughter, a single parent raising a son and dealing with the same loss. My son Ced is strong, silent, and hurt. My baby girl Lee is so beautiful and bright. Being the positive light she's always been publicly, but in private, she still cries. I hear the conversations she still has with her big brother. He encourages her to turn her pain into passion because that's her purpose. So I hear her say my wounds are pushing me into wealth. I'm helpless at this moment, frozen with guilt and a million questions.

I'M LOST, AND ONLY YOU CAN DELIVER ME FROM THE DEPTH OF MY DESPAIR.

7/24/2019

I'm weary and wrought with conflicting emotions. Overcome with self-pity and holding on to bitterness and a hurt so deep the pain surpasses any words. My eyes fill up and run over, but this time, it doesn't relieve my pain. I miss my son, and nothing gives me comfort, no words, no cliches, knowing the spirit never dies, nothing. God, I need your help. I need the same God that loaned my baby to me to love, the same God that spared his life, the same God that gave him favor, the same God that kept him for all those years to show up now and give me peace. I'm lost, and only You can deliver me from the depth of my despair.

_____

_____

_____

_____

_____

_____

_____

_____

_____

_____

_____

_____

_____

_____

_____

_____

_____

_____

_____

_____

_____

TODAY WOULD HAVE BEEN YOUR 39TH BIRTHDAY

October 4, 2019

Today would have been your 39th birthday, but you're no longer in this dimension. The emptiness feels like "where are you?", "when will you be back?", "come home."

Bargaining like "just one more day" rather, "one more minute" (the longest 60 seconds ever).

In the midst of that, there is a flashback that it was done. All there was for the person to do was done. Just didn't know what I was witnessing.

It's like the worst breakup ever. The relationship you didn't see ending, no unraveling. Just one day, it's over.

How to not remember and feel all the connections and reminders—turning those reminders from sadness to gratitude because it happened. Life happened. Thank God. What a life without them would be. I never want to know what a life without them ever existing would be . . . I never want to know.

I am grateful for the time. I selfishly want more. But all I had was such a gift. I'd never want less.

When your world changes, it changes you. Admitting the pain is therapeutic. It helps release it, so I think. Our love will never end.

Troy Lee, I love you sooooo.

My Tears Didn't Change God's Mind!

_____

_____

_____

_____

_____

_____

_____

_____

_____

_____

_____

_____

_____

_____

_____

_____

_____

_____

_____

_____

Rose Greer

DEATH IS BITTER.

October 4, 2019

The hurt today is even more painful than yesterday. Today you should have celebrated your 39th birthday, but instead, we released lanterns hoping they could reach you in heaven. I'm angry with God for taking you away from me. No amount of condolences lessens the hurt. I'm screaming on the inside, and hot tears make their way down my cheeks that no longerglow. I'm screaming, but God obviously doesn't hear me, or He simply has turned his face from me. I'm screaming for just one more day, one hour or one minute. Screaming because this morning, your dad said today my son would be 39. Screaming because the day you left, I lost you, your children, and your dad. Death is bitter.

REMINDED OF LOSS

October 7, 2019

What an amazing weekend of celebration, appreciation, and remembrance of him. He touched so many. Just amazing. So proud of who he was and continues to be to everyone. Blessed to be impacted by him during his lifetime here.

I couldn't imagine the emotional toll this would have on the family. Essentially three days ... we had three services for my son, and it was ... hard ... reopened wounds ... reminded of loss and ache for him ...

_____

_____

_____

_____

_____

_____

_____

_____

_____

_____

_____

_____

_____

_____

_____

_____

_____

_____

_____

_____

COPING IS ONE MOMENT AT A TIME.

October 8, 2019

The emptiness feels like "where are you" "when will you be back" "come home"

Bargaining like "just one more day" rather "one more minute"

In the midst of that, there is a flashback that it was done. All there was for you to do was done. Just didn't know what I was witnessing

It's like the worst breakup ever. The relationship you didn't see ending, no unraveling. Just one day it's over.

How do I not remember you're gone and feel all the lost connections?

Life happened to me. Thank God. What is life without you? I never wanted to know Coping is One moment at a time.

_____

_____

_____

_____

_____

_____

_____

_____

_____

_____

_____

_____

_____

_____

_____

_____

_____

_____

_____

_____

_____

THE GOD I SERVED TOOK YOU AWAY.

October 11. 2019

They say your sadness should soon turn to gratitude because of the time I was blessed with you. That hasn't happened to me. I still feel like you were snatched from me with no warning. The God I served took you away. He didn't ask. He didn't care that I would bury a piece of me with you. He didn't care that I was a giver, a good person, and a Christian. No, not one thought was given for those of us that loved you.

My Tears Didn't Change God's Mind!

_____
_____
_____
_____
_____
_____
_____
_____
_____
_____
_____
_____
_____
_____
_____
_____
_____
_____
_____
_____
_____

Rose Greer

WHAT DO I FILL UP THAT EMPTY HOLE WITH?

October 12, 2019

I'm screaming I love you! I miss you! You have no idea how much just us talking for a few minutes meant to me! I feel

like I didn't appreciate you.

My loss, my pain . . . is like when someone takes a knife and cuts out the inside of a watermelon . . . What do I fill up that empty hole with?

October 13, 2019

I was robbed and defrauded of any choice in this matter.

GOD HELP ME, PLEASE.

October 14, 2019

Now I'm running, trying to catch myself. Trying to figure out what's next. I've lost my son, my husband, and my business has suffered tremendously while I've battled depression. To make my shortcomings appear even more prominent, my mom just told me she has gotten a job to make ends meet.

God help me, please.

God's word promises to give us the grace necessary to successfully deal with the circumstances we are facing. He is not a God who withholds goodness and mercy. He will strengthen us and reestablish our peace. Psalm 84:11 For the Lord God is a sun and shield; the Lord will give grace and glory.

SOCIAL MEDIA POST FROM YOUR SISTER
LEEANNGREER

IG:leelee1908

Block out your fear, Tackle your problems head on and Finish strong.

Everyday love sees me through the dark.

Truth is I dread special occasions because you can feel the hole in our family... I know I'll never stop missing my brother. I just hope I find some normalcy in this. I'm still waiting for you to come back... LeeAnn Greer

October 15, 2019

I'm alone, but God is NOT absent.
He is in the pain; He is in the sorrow.

October 16, 2019

Looking in the mirror, telling myself, "Stop repeating the pain of yesterday. Just Stop it! It's hindering me, controlling me, stopping me from becoming. The pain of my loss is defining my today."

My Tears Didn't Change God's Mind!

_____

_____

_____

_____

_____

_____

_____

_____

_____

_____

_____

_____

_____

_____

_____

_____

_____

_____

November 1, 2019

I was a prayer warrior, seed sower, minister, and a prophet.
And God let my well run dry.

November 2, 2019

I'm at the darkest, coldest season in my life, and God continues to call me. Why would I answer? When He turned a deaf ear to my cry.

_____
_____
_____
_____
_____
_____
_____
_____
_____
_____
_____
_____
_____
_____
_____
_____
_____
_____
_____
_____

November 3, 2019

Today trusting God would be a superpower.

November 11, 2019

Nothing is going right. The conversations in my head are all over the place. I've tried over and over again to quiet the voice that keeps trying to convince me the hurt would stop if I'd simply stop breathing. Give up, just quit because I'm no good for anyone anymore. It seems pretty simple, but the voice of reason says everything will get better, all of the hurt will heal, the losses will turn into wins, the lack will turn into abundance. Where is God while my humanness is threatening my life? Where was God the day my son's heart stopped beating? Where was God when my sun stopped shining? Where was God when my baby boy decided to quell his hurt by drinking or when my baby girl decided to work 18 hours a day so she wouldn't have time to think, or when Pumpkin became angry at the world because her brother and best friend are no longer here? Where are you God as I wear the scars of losing my son on my face? Where are you omnipresent God as the grief threatens my life?

Thanksgiving 2019

My first one without you. Tronicka, Ced, and Lee are struggling to be without you here. No words can define the pain we are experiencing, and nothing or no one can replace you. I have more questions today than I had the day you left. God seems to ignore all of them. I heard LeeAnn say she doesn't want to be here

without you. That broke my heart even more.

How could one person be sooooo loved?

I don't know how but you are.

I'm boarding a plane to Phoenix. They say you can hear God clearly there and find healing and peace. Please son, send me a message to help me help them and myself.

The capacity to rescue my husband, my children, or my grandchildren from this loss doesn't exist. So today, I run away from my family, but there is no escaping my thoughts.

GOD, YOU SAID YOU'D NEVER LEAVE ME NOR FORSAKE ME.

December 2019

How could this be? No warning, No time for goodbye. Standing here while my heart lies on the floor, wondering where my heartbeat went. When did my lungs decide not to breathe anymore? God, you said you'd never leave me nor forsake me. In this moment, you've left, and I feel forever forsaken. My everything is screaming Noooooooooooooo, this didn't happen to me. I thought I was chosen, called, appointed, and of course, favored. When did that stop? No words; tomorrow just never came.

TODAY I REALIZED MY GRIEF WILL NEVER END.

December 13, 2019

Today I realized my grief will never end. Because grief is just displaced love. You can't love others more to lessen the hurt; you can't forget that there was a you here in the flesh. I can't erase my memories of you, nor do I want to. I can't fill the empty space in my heart with someone else. No, grief never ends when it's the flesh of your flesh, bone of your bone, love that grew from the depth of my soul. So now that I've accepted that this is my fate. I move forward, praying for a good day today.

December 24th

I love you forever and always . . . until we meet again!

CHAPTER

5

DEPRESSION IS REAL, AND IT HURTS

All I could feel was darkness. For the first 12 months, I wore black every day. I was lifeless. I literally wore my grief. I was the portrait in the flesh of death daily. I was a mother in mourning, and the darkness I felt on the inside was revealed as my reality on the outside. It was indescribable and unexplainable, but it was evident when you saw me. Grief and its depth are real. There's a concept that you grieve as deep as you love. I've found that statement to be true and painful.

People's theory that Christians and black people don't suffer from suicidal thoughts and mental illness is a lie; it's just not talked about. There are mental health issues that come from grief. Your health is affected by grief. Many people will watch you go through the motions and have their sarcastic, judgmental opinions of the things you are doing, but no one will ever understand unless they have to walk a day in your shoes. Your coping mechanism may not be like others, and in grief, there is no sense of comparison as each person grieves in their own way.

As a result of my pain, I wouldn't eat. Sugar was my fix, and weight gain became my portion. Prior to my loss, I was a fitness freak. I would exercise daily, however, at this point, exercise wasn't a thought, and eating right didn't even exist. I tried all kinds of things to fill the void, ease the pain, and hopefully wake me up from the worst nightmare ever. However, some things were a waste of time, some temporal, and some an interesting experience, but they all were a part of me trying to pick up the pieces.

I tried tapping sessions, hot yoga; I went to the prophets, called for the mediums, even went through four psychiatrists as a result of suffering from Broken Heart Syndrome. Broken Heart Syndrome, as I call it, is when you think you want to live, but your mind is telling your body no. I won't say that some things didn't help because they did in one sense or another. I can truly appreciate my last therapist. She was forthcoming with me. She said, "I can't fix you, but I can hear you. I will help you learn to cope in order to live with your loss." I liked her. She didn't lie to me. She didn't give me false hope; she gave me the truth. The other psychiatrists would tell me what to do and what they would fix. My rebuttal was, "the only way you can fix this is to bring my son back. What time are you making this happen?"

I literally wanted to die. I didn't think I would still be here now. I had given up my will to live. I remember calling my psychiatrist and telling her I was going to play in traffic on the freeway behind where my job was. Her response was, "Rose, I don't think that's a good idea." My response was, "It's the best one I have today." It's funny now how she asked if I took my medicine (I call them my crazy lady pills) that day. I was like, "Um, the medicine that makes me forget my name? Well no, I forgot to take it." These were real moments for me.

Some days I had really checked out. It was as if no one else existed, just emptiness. I remember Thanksgiving Day 2019. I got up without prior planning, went to the airport, and caught a flight to Sedona, Arizona. I was unhinged. The healing mountains were in Sedona, and they say you can hear the voice of God there. I was looking for a word. I was really looking to meet my son there, hoping he would return, but he never did. I encountered so many highs and lows. I had sporadic crying spells on and off. I can remember one day sitting in the closet crying for 11 hours straight, overcome with grief and pain. Depression had a hold on me to the point I didn't realize how it was affecting everyone else. My husband had checked on his position as a husband, provider, and father. He no longer had a passion to experience life or family. My kids were trying to hold it together in their own ways and nurse me to life at the same time. I applaud my kids for their tenacity to keep me from dying too. I was hurting. They saw it, felt it, and even though they may never say it, they were affected by it. It wasn't my desire to hurt, neglect, or burden them. It was my desire to anesthetize the pain.

People are walking around depressed every day, and their coping mechanisms have become the daily gossip and judgment call for many. I admonish you if you've never experienced grief or loss; please, by all means, have compassion on those you see overtaken with depression and anxiety. It's not the action that needs the most attention; it's the pain.

SILENCED

I pulled the trigger . . . No longer in my imagination and abstract but front and center fully intact I pulled that trigger. I asked myself over and over again why I fought this torment. Why can't I just make it end? Still looking for the temperament to take down this tornado conceived of pain, rage, and these misguided feelings. I have created a melody composed of hurt, humiliation, and hostility. As the ballot plays, this world starts to cave, and not realizing I'm sending us to our graves, we're past the point of no return now, it's too late. It doesn't hurt anymore . . . I apologize you couldn't see it. My poker face was pure perfection. I created it to stand up to all scrutinies. I kept the truth buried deep inside of me. In this world, I am no longer. There's nothing left of me to give. But worry not, and please try to forget how I left. Honor me by remembering me and how I lived this life. I know at times you may be saddened, but don't worry for me, for if you look within the depths of your soul, there I shall be.

By Yanna Young

CHAPTER

6

THEY WOULDN'T
LET ME DIE

If I could just stop breathing, everything would be okay. When you die, everything is perfect. You go back to the original creation. The thought of me, broken and empty was devastating. My perfect self was the epitome of a happy life. I had a loving, growing family, four healthy, beautiful kids, a successful, thriving business, and great relationships.

Now I have PTSD, suffering from depression, on anxiety meds, blood pressure pills, and I can't speak about my son without tears.

I didn't look like I had suicidal thoughts. It didn't look like I had anxiety, but I was dying and wanted to die.

My kids had to bring me to the ER on several occasions. Heart rate and blood pressure steadily dropping. My mind was consumed with grief, and my body was shutting down. I clearly remember taking 29 blood pressure pills. I was lying there lifeless and ready to die. I didn't choose to live. I was choosing to die by way of overdose. I remember the doctor told me that day that I had a choice. I could choose to survive and learn to cope with my loss, or I could choose to die and leave the rest of those that needed me behind. I can honestly say that day, I didn't choose to live, but I chose to think about the process.

I can remember Troy Lee's spirit standing me up and telling me it wasn't my time to die. I told him I needed him here, and his response was, "I am here more with you now, than I was before." He told me, "I'm still present. I'm just here in a different dimension."

At that point, I chose to think about my choice. Suicide is selfish, but you don't realize it. You don't really realize anything when you are consumed with unbelief, betrayal, anger, fear, and hopelessness. You just want to feel normal again.

I had to realize, it would NEVER be normal again. I'm going to forever have an issue because my son is never coming back.

The words of my baby boy forever echo in my head. He says, "Mom, everyone has a contract. Troy Lee's contract has ended." The soberness in this is knowing that God knows my brokenness. I was surprised at my loss, but God wasn't.

Troy Lee was only loaned to me.

CHAPTER

7

THE NEW
NORMAL

I can sum up my emotions by using the statement "healing but no wholeness". Will I ever be whole again? I'm not sure, but I'm learning to cope. Will it get better? No. Does it get easier? No. However, I understand I need to be present.

In my quest, I can understand why some people go off what others consider the "deep end" from whatever their norm was. Some run off and travel the world, some resort to alcohol, drugs, senseless relationships, loveless feats or behaviors, gambling, etc. All because they are trying to figure out how to cope. They are depressed, broken, empty, lost, shattered, and they are trying to navigate through their loss and devastation. While everyone else is still in their norm, they are trying to adapt to their new normal.

What does a new normal look like? How do you continue life when someone who is normally there is no longer present in the family photos? What's normal about the life of the party being absent at family gatherings? How do you embrace the new normal?

I'm learning to cope without anxiety and sleeping pills. I'm learning to cope by talking about it. I'm learning to cope while writing this book, encouraging you to breathe again.

One day at a time. One step at a time. One gesture at a time.

You can live; it's just a new normal. Does it take some adjusting? Yes. Is it uncomfortable? Yes. Can it be beautiful? I believe it can. Matter of fact, I know it can because Troy Lee is my biggest cheerleader. He's walking me through this entire process. He is constantly letting me know what I can do and what can be accomplished. He told me this is necessary for me and those that will read this.

It's forever sobering knowing that Troy Lee is sheer perfection now. He no longer has the third and fourth-degree burns that he had since two years old. They are gone now because he was made perfect in Christ. This is what God intended, and at some point, I'm learning to be content in this current state I am in. To this day, Troy Lee encourages me. I believe he is here with me in spirit. Many don't believe in life being present after death, but Troy Lee is not dead. He's here with me in spirit. The truth is God allowed Troy Lee to be the first person to change my life drastically upon his entrance into the world. Well, he has done it again. He has transformed my life drastically with his departure.

CHAPTER

8

SMALL STEPS LEAD
TO BIG CHANGES

When suffering a major loss, we go through stages of emotions and are constantly looking for different ways to cope and manage the emotions we are trying to compartmentalize. This chapter is dedicated to suggestive and tried methods that lead to a sense of comfort. Healing, closure, and comfort don't happen overnight, but it comes one step at a time.

THE PHASE OF DENIAL

1. **Buy a nice notebook.** This will help with the transitioning process. Journaling is not a new phenomenon, but only recently it has been proven to help people work through complex feelings. Journaling worked for me as a way to process my thoughts and feelings surrounding the death of my son. I'll have to admit, I was a little skeptical at first. But pouring my feelings into the journal was

therapeutic. It didn't make my feelings go away overnight, but it did help me to begin to sift through my emotions.

2. **A comforting memory of my loved one is . . .** Journaling prompts can be a great idea to help you get started. I will include some of my favorite ones in this book as part of the activity sections. If you feel an urge to write about something else, then please go ahead and write what feels right to you. Just getting your feelings down on paper can be a great help.

3. **Get some fresh air.** Whether you go for a walk around the block or whether you spend a little time in your backyard, it doesn't matter. Just do what feels right to you, but if you are able to, get yourself outside. When you are outside, try taking some deep breaths of fresh air. It can help us to feel more grounded in the moment.

4. **Cross something off your to-do list.** When a loved one has passed on, your to-do list can get longer and longer. This can often lead to you feeling even more overwhelmed. The process of crossing just one thing off that list, no matter what it is, can really help you to feel a little more positive.

5. **I find it helpful when . . .** This is another prompt for your journal. Having these prompts, rather than just writing down all of your many feelings, helps you to organize your thoughts, which in turn helps you to get more out of journaling.

6. **Take a nap.** Self-care during such a difficult period in your life can often take the back burner, but no matter how you are feeling, taking care of yourself is key. Remember, you can't pour from an empty cup. Even if you don't manage to sleep, just having an hour of quiet time can give you more energy to get on with your day.

7. **Write a positive affirmation down.** Choose a quote you resonate with, write it down and display it somewhere you will see it often. Maybe on the bathroom mirror or on the fridge. There are plenty of quotes out there that can help you through the loss of a loved one. Even writing something such as, "You are strong," can help you to believe it.

8. **Write a letter to your loved one.** No matter what you are feeling at this stage, writing a letter to your loved one can help with the grieving process. Whether you are angry with them for leaving or sad about the loss, writing your feelings down on paper can really help you out.

9. **Take some deep breaths.** Take a moment to concentrate on your breathing. Slowly in and out. Notice where you hold the breath. Can you feel it moving through your body? This is a mindfulness technique to help you quiet your mind a little. It can be useful to try this out when you become overwhelmed.

10. **I wish somebody would say . . .** This is another great journal prompt to help you sort through your feelings. By thinking about how we would like to be helped, we can allow others to support us in our grief. Remember, supporting somebody else through grief is a tricky process, so if we are able to share with others what support we need, this can really be helpful.

11. **Plant some flowers, or water your plants.** Taking care of something else during the grieving process, even if it's simply a plant or flower, can help you to regain some focus. If you can, spend a moment to simply be with the plant. Be present in the moment with the sensations, the smells.

12. **Visualise a memory of your loved one. Write it into your journal using your five senses: touch, taste, smell, hearing, and sight.** The memory can be anything at all. Happy, sad, or anything in between. It doesn't even have to be a particularly special memory. Getting in touch with your senses is an ideal way to begin to process the loss of a loved one.

13. **If you're religious, pray.** If you're not religious, take some time to talk to the universe or any other higher power you believe in. Our beliefs and religion can often take a back seat after the loss of a loved one, especially if you are having some contentious thoughts about the religion as a result of the loss (which is perfectly normal). So taking a little time to try to reconnect with your faith, whatever that may be, can help you begin to process your feelings.

14. **Try an adult coloring book or jigsaw.** Yes, this might sound a little silly, but it can help to distract your mind for a little while. Focusing all of your energy on the death of a loved one is not always positive. Our mind needs to take a break sometimes, and activities such as these can help with this, distracting your mind for even just an hour or so.

15. **Pick up a book.** Similar to the last point, reading can be a great form of escape, and often escape is what we crave after the loss of a loved one. Getting away from our lives, and lost in the pages of a book, is ideal during this time in your life. If you're having trouble concentrating on a book, which is completely normal, why not try a magazine or newspaper instead?

These activities are aimed at the beginning or the first few months following the loss of a loved one (or whatever loss you are experiencing). During the beginning of your loss, we often find ourselves in denial, which is entirely normal. This stage may last a little longer than others or may be shorter. During this time, our raw emotions take over. We still haven't come to terms with the loss, and our emotions feel muddled and confused. As we begin to move into the next phase of our lives, after the loss, our emotions might become a little clearer. Often, at this stage, we find ourselves leaning towards anger and resentment.

Rose Greer

THE PHASE OF ANGER

1. **When I feel angry, it helps to remember . . .** Let's start off with a journal prompt about anger. Journaling through all the emotions associated with loss can help you to sort through your feelings and find clarity. Identifying what helps you to push through feelings of anger will support you the next time you feel angry.

2. **Listen to some music.** Whether you fancy listening to some nostalgic music or some recent pop music, music is a great way to help us feel present in the moment. If you feel like it, sing and dance. Something that helped me was listening to my son's favorite music. It helped me to feel close to him in the months following his loss, even though it was music I would never have normally listened to.

3. **Hug somebody you love.** Hug your partner, your mother, your children, even your pets. Hugging releases serotonin that helps us to feel happier and less angry. It can be easy to take our anger out on those around us, and so showing we care, in this case through a hug, can help us to feel more positive.

4. **I feel guilty/ashamed about . . .** Journaling isn't just for positive emotions. Writing our negative emotions down on paper can help us to understand how we feel. Remember that however you feel is valid. No matter what you are feeling, feel it. Feelings of guilt can often arise after the loss of a loved one, and many of us struggle to articulate these feelings to others. Writing them down gets the thoughts out of your brain and onto paper, helping you to move towards a more positive mindset (which I know is easier said than done).

5. **Look at photographs of your loved one.** Sometimes, when we are grieving, we try to distance ourselves from the pain and try to avoid seeing reminders of our loved one. This is a completely normal part of the grieving process. However, looking back through photographs and memories of your loved one can be incredibly beneficial. Ignoring emotions, even though this often makes the loss easier in the short term, can prolong the pain. Take a little time to look back and remember the happy times you had. Remember the sad times too. Just remember.

6. **Get moving.** Whatever your exercise preference is, try to make some time for it and get your body moving. Whether you choose to watch exercise videos on YouTube, or visit the gym, or even just go for a walk, exercise will help you to feel more grounded. Exercise releases endorphins that will help you to forget about your anger for a little while, which can be a welcome break for many of us.

7. **I no longer want to feel this anger. I would love to feel . . .** This sneaky little journal prompt is aimed to help you start to imagine what you would like your future to be like. It doesn't put too much pressure on you to imagine your 'new normal', but rather asks you to focus on how you hope to feel in the future.

8. **Unplug from the world for a while.** Social media is often more of a hindrance than a help during grief and so logging out of your Facebook or Instagram accounts might be a good idea. Give yourself permission to ignore phone calls and texts that you don't want to answer to (for a little while, anyway). The world will not stop because you don't answer a text. Take some time away from electronics and focus on the physical world around you.

9. **Rearrange a room in your house.** Linking back to the previous idea, rearranging a room in your house helps you to get in touch with the physical world around you. It can help you to feel more in control and calmer. Even if your house is tidy and clutter-free, the simple act of rearranging furniture can help you to feel more positive and present.

10. **Write a list of the people you love and why you love them.** Feeling grateful for what we have in our lives can be difficult, if not impossible, after the loss of a loved one. But, hopefully, you have people in your lives that you love and who love you in return. This is something to celebrate. Writing a list of who you can rely on helps you to focus on the good aspects of your life. As we often get dragged down into negative feelings—depression, sadness, anger, denial—after the loss of somebody we love, trying to move the focus onto something else can help you to feel a little better.

11. **Visit a support group or join an online forum for grief.** This is a tricky step to take. I remember how hard it was to seek help. Putting yourself out there during such a difficult period in your life is one of the toughest things anybody can do. But hearing other people's stories, and talking about your own, if you feel able to, can help you to gain perspective. We can become very 'shut in' after grief—literally and figuratively—and venturing out into the world can be a difficult but incredibly worthwhile thing to do.

12. **Dear Anger . . .** Write a letter to your anger. This might sound a little silly, but writing a letter to your anger can help you to process why you are feeling angry. Yes, you are angry because your loved one has passed, but you might have other reasons to be angry. There might

have even been some reasons for your anger that have been sitting just below the surface for a long time. Getting to the root cause can be so beneficial, as you will be able to work through those feelings so much better once you know what they are and why they are there.

13. **Quality time with a loved one.** After the loss of a loved one, we can find that we withdraw from those around us for many different reasons. Maybe we struggle to communicate our feelings, or they remind us too much of our loved one. But taking that step and deciding to spend time with the people in your life that you love can be such a welcome break from the anger or any other emotion, you are feeling.

14. **Get creative.** Draw, paint, doodle, collage. Being creative can take our minds away from our anger and help us to process our feelings. A great tip is to create a picture that shows how you are feeling. Give your feelings a form—choose colors and mediums that show your feelings. This is something that many therapists use with people processing grief, particularly children, and that makes it all the more important for you to try out. You don't have to be an artist to put your feelings down on paper (or any other background) in a creative way.

15. **Yoga, yoga, yoga!** Yoga is a great way to de-stress and work through feelings of anger and resentment. The stretches and breathing techniques are all about making your body and mind feel good. Yoga can help you to regroup and rinse out any negative energy. If you haven't tried yoga before, I guarantee you even a simple ten-minute stretch will help you to feel good. There are loads of videos on YouTube to try out for people of all ages and flexibilities.

The main aim of these activities is to help you process your feelings and get back out into the world, in your own time, of course. There is no time limit on how long you are allowed to grieve, and putting yourself first during this time is perfectly okay. Feelings of guilt around this are normal, and hopefully, the steps above help you to begin to feel able to process how you are feeling and allow you to cope with your feelings. Try out the ones you fancy doing and feel able to. If there are some you don't think are for you, then that's perfectly fine too. The important thing is that you are doing little things every single day to help you process your feelings and work towards the new normal. The one thing I suggest you do, even if you don't particularly feel like it, is journaling. Just try it out a few times; it was an absolute Godsend for me.

THE PHASE OF BARGAINING

1. **Tell a story about your loved one.** Whether you wish to tell the story aloud to somebody else, or write it in your journal, talking (or writing) about your loved one can help with the healing process.

2. **Read a non-fiction book.** There are loads of choices out there, from memoirs to self-help. Non-fiction books can help you to take a moment for yourself. We all need a break sometimes, and this is the perfect opportunity for that break.

3. **Watch a movie.** Any movie will do. If you want to stay home and get curled up on the couch, maybe with your friends or family, then go for it. Or, if you want to get out of the house, go to your local cinema. Movies are a great form of escapism, and sometimes we just need to escape.

4. **Write a letter to yourself from your loved one.** This might seem strange at first, but often after we lose somebody that we love, we imagine what they would say to us. We might even still have conversations with them. Taking the time to write a letter from your loved one to you is often an ideal way to work through your feelings.

5. **I feel hopeful about . . . I feel hopeless about . . .** These are two sides of the same coin, so to speak. During the months following the loss of a loved one, we can feel like things are outside of our control. Make a list of the things you feel hopeful/hopeless about. You might find there's more to be hopeful about than you first thought.

6. **Write your loved one's name in the middle of a blank page.** Surround it with all the words you associate with them. Positive and negative words are welcome here. It is normal to feel angry with a loved one for leaving us behind, and writing in your journal is a

positive way to work through these emotions. Similarly, filling the page with words that make you think of your loved one can be a great memorial exercise. It can help you to remember and cherish the past.

7. **Today, I am thankful for . . .** This is often a lot easier than you would think. When we lose a loved one, it leaves a huge hole in our lives. We know that our lives will be forever changed, but that doesn't mean there aren't things to be thankful for. Maybe it's a lovely sunny day. Maybe you have a supportive person in your life. Maybe you've got a roof over your head. Whatever you are thankful for, write it down. Write as many as you can. It might also be useful to keep that list handy. Pin it to the fridge or put it in the drawer of your bedside table. It can be useful to remind ourselves of what we have to be thankful for, especially when our world seems like a dark place.

8. **Take a short break.** If you are able to, get out of the house for a few days. It doesn't matter if you go to the Bahamas or simply an hour down the road. Getting out of the house will help you to feel centered. It can be useful to break up the routine you are in, especially if you've noticed that you're struggling to go about your daily life. Whether you go with your partner, your children, your friends, or alone, taking a short break will likely do you a world of good.

9. **Describe how your loved one died.** Yes, I know this could seem detrimental. But writing factually about their death—where, how, why it happened—can help you to progress towards accepting the 'new normal' in your life. This one is a bit of a double-edged sword as, if you are ready for this step, it can really help you to make

progress in managing your grief and emotions. If you are not ready or have trauma around the event, then please give this one a pass, for now at least.

10. **Do something you used to enjoy.** This could be something you used to enjoy before the passing of your loved one, or even something you enjoyed doing as a child. Things can get put on the backburner during grief when instead, we should try to continue to do the things we used to enjoy. Maybe this is having a long bath or going to the swimming pool. It doesn't matter, just make the time to do something that you enjoy.

11. **Check in with your loved ones.** Hopefully, your family and friends have been supportive throughout your grieving process. Make the time to check in with them and ask how they are doing. Showing that you love and appreciate them for supporting you through your grief can, in turn, help you to feel a little brighter, too, especially if you have been experiencing feelings of guilt.

12. **How have you changed since the loss of your loved one?** This diary prompt is often difficult. You might initially want to jump on negatives about how you believe you've changed, but I challenge you to think of some positive ways you have changed. Maybe you're a lot stronger than you realized, or you have learned to accept your feelings. Plus, anything you put as a negative, I would guarantee that nearly everybody else experiencing grief noticed too. You're not alone, and you don't have to be at your best 100% of the time.

13. **Try something you've never done before.** I've left this one open-ended for you as there are so many possibilities. It doesn't need to be anything extreme. I'm not suggesting that you go skydiving or run a marathon (unless that's what you want to do). It could be something

like trying new food, getting a massage or getting a piercing. As long as it is something you've never done before, go nuts.

14. **I can honor you by . . .** This is a lovely journal prompt to get you motivated for your future. You might not be ready to think too far in advance just yet, and that's fine. But think of ways you can honor the memory of your loved one. It could be something as simple as to continue living and being present. Maybe you want to write a book. Or, maybe they were passionate about something, and you could find a way to use this to honor them. The possibilities are almost endless here.

15. **My biggest grief trigger is . . .** As you experience grief, you might begin to notice that there are some aspects of your life that trigger grief more than others. Maybe it's being around a certain person or a certain place. It could be when you're alone. Being mindful about what your triggers are is useful because you will learn to cope in those situations. You can't change things if you're not aware of what needs to be changed, after all.

Remember, dealing with grief is not a linear process. Some days will be better than others. I hope that these ideas for journal prompts and activities will help you to move beyond bargaining and towards accepting the death of your loved one. This is an incredibly difficult thing to do, and it will happen in your own time. You might never fully accept that this is your reality now, but you can learn to live with it, and these activities are there to help you get yourself back out there and learn how to cope with your 'new normal'.

THE PHASE OF ACCEPTANCE

1. **Start by recording your joys.** Every single day I want you to write down what good things have happened to you. What made you joyful today? Maybe you saw somebody being kind to an elderly person, and that made you smile. Maybe you washed your comforter. It doesn't have to be anything major or significant. Recording all of the 'joys' you experience helps you to have a more positive outlook on life. All of the little joys add up. Never underestimate the power of developing a positive mindset.

2. **Laugh!** Do something that makes you laugh, whether it's watching funny animal videos on the internet or watching a comedian on the TV (or even in real life if you're able to). You might not initially feel like doing something that makes you laugh if you are feeling down, but it can certainly help out.

3. **Meditation and mindfulness.** I've briefly mentioned meditation in other sections of this book. I think it can be a great support throughout the whole grieving process, but for now, all I would like you to do is find a quiet place and sit in a comfy position. Take a moment to quiet your mind. Now, tighten and release each muscle in your body one at a time. Start at your toes and work your way to the very top of your head. Take your time. Repeat if needed.

4. **Do something to make somebody else smile.** Small acts of kindness go a long way. If you're out getting coffee, pay for the drink of the person behind you. Buy a homeless person a meal. Buy some flowers for somebody you know (or a stranger if you're feeling brave). These small acts of kindness put some well-needed positive energy back into the world while also making you feel a little bit better too. Bonus!

5. **Write 15 things you love about yourself.** This is a brilliant way to get you looking at yourself in a positive light again. Working through your depression is all about trying to find that positivity that is hidden within you. Bullet journal prompts such as this will help you to begin to look on the bright side again.

6. **Write a letter forgiving yourself for a past mistake.** This one is a tricky one, let me tell you. But it certainly helps you to work through any guilt, depression, anger, or denial you might still have bottled up. To overcome these feelings, you have to process them and move on, which is easier said than done, I know. However, a simple journal prompt such as this can be the start to helping you look towards the future and see it in a more positive light.

7. **Send a thank you note.** Writing a little thank you note on paper and sending it to somebody whom you wish to thank can really help to boost your mood. Letting somebody know how much you appreciate them puts happiness into the world and gives a little back to you too.

8. **Spend some time in the sunshine.** Whether you spend fifteen minutes in your own backyard or you visit the beach, spending some time outdoors in the sun can help you to feel a little brighter. Remember, this section is all about moving through any depression and sadness you might be feeling. Never underestimate the power of Vitamin D!

9. **Have a get-together with friends and family.** This is especially great if your friends and family knew your loved one who has passed. It can be a great time to share stories and celebrate their life, especially as everybody there will be in the same boat in terms of grieving for the loved one. Sharing in your grief, whilst a tricky thing to start,

it can be so therapeutic once the floodgates open, and everybody is sharing and being supportive.

10. **Visit a place of natural beauty.** In previous sections, I've mentioned that spending time in nature can help you to feel happier and more positive. Visiting a place of natural beauty, whether that be mountains, woodlands, the beach, or a lake, can help you to find a better head-space. Spend some time admiring the beauty around you.

11. **Write a letter to your younger self.** Tell them everything you wish you had known back then. Be brutally honest and don't hold back. Is there any advice you could give yourself to help you better navigate life and losing your loved one? This little task can help you to put things into perspective. We often find it easier to give others advice, and distancing yourself from your past self might help you help yourself.

12. **Take some time getting ready.** Spend a little longer getting ready in the morning or evening, whether you're going out or not. Wash your hair and spend time cleansing your body. Then, treat yourself to a squirt of aftershave or perfume. If you want to, put some makeup on and style your hair. It might sound a little vain but looking good helps us to feel good. There's no harm in spending time taking care of yourself. You don't have to do this every day, but it can be a big mood-booster every so often.

13. **Something you taught me . . .** Whether this is an actual skill or a life lesson, for this journal prompt, think about what your loved one gave to you that will help you with the rest of your life. Try to practice gratitude here, thanking them for what they have done for you, rather than focusing on the loss. During the Winter of Loss,

we are trying to look forward to the rest of our lives, and practicing gratitude for the time we had with our loved one is the perfect place to start.

14. **Write a poem or short story.** We've already mentioned that being creative can help with the healing process. As we move into our future, creativity can help us to process any leftover feelings from the previous year. Write a poem or short story, either for or about your loved one, that you would like to share with them. Remember, poems don't have to rhyme!

15. **Visit a place your loved one visited.** Your loved one may have had a preferred coffee shop, park, or animal shelter. Choose a place that means something to them and visit it. Spend some time absorbing the atmosphere and remembering the good times you've had with your loved one. Whether it's a place you both used to visit together or if it's somewhere completely brand new to you, this is a perfect activity to help you heal and accept your 'new normal' going forward.

We know that grieving is not a straightforward process. The emotions we face regularly change, and just when we think we are healing and ready to continue with our lives, we are thrown a curveball. Unfortunately, that's just part of grief. Hopefully, the activities and journal prompts I've included in this section will help you to progress. The idea is that they will help you to experience more feelings of hopefulness and positivity rather than focusing on the loss. You will always feel the loss of your loved one that will never go away. But that doesn't mean that your life has to end too. You can still find purpose and positivity, even when life seems to have dealt you a poor hand.

9

THE PRELUDE
TO PURPOSE

How is purpose really made evident in our lives? How do you come to know and accept what you were put on this earth to do or even experience? Before Troy Lee transitioned, I thought I had arrived. I just knew God was pleased, and my life was making an impact by my presentation. I had this perfect plan and blueprint for my future. Sure I knew there was more to my life that I had never tapped into yet. Certainly, I knew God wanted to use me in a greater capacity for Him to be glorified. What I didn't know was how He would do it, especially if I didn't voluntarily put my hands to it. If God had told me, I'm going to take your son to birth your purpose, I would have done everything in my ability to spare him. I would have tried to keep everything perfect. I would have scotch guarded us to prevent the unforeseen from coming into existence.

However, somehow as Troy Lee's spirit is with me and the spirit of God is carrying me through this process, I can't help but believe that even in my loss, grief, pain, anger, resentment, feelings of betrayal, suicide, and emptiness that I have stumbled into purpose. I've felt a pain that many have been unable to articulate. I've experienced anguish that many aren't able to identify. I've sat in a seat that no one signs up for, and yet where I once wanted to end it all, I find myself hopeful. I'm hopeful because I can help those that still feel what I felt. I can encourage us that we can live beyond loss.

This time a year ago, I thought my life was over. I believed death was my lot. What I didn't realize was that the me I created had to die to become the me God created to live. Do I still miss Troy Lee? Every day my heart longs for him. However, every day I can see a little clearer. I can identify what others look over, are passive about, and have no empathy for; and I can embrace it and say, you're gonna make it. I thought I had lost my first love, but in his absence, the same love has ushered me back to life. Love in its infinite form resurrected my spirit, and it's the same love that will resurrect you too. Seeing past your reality isn't easy, but if you can just get a deeper glimpse, you'll begin to heal and live again.

I want to pray for you.

Father in the name of Jesus, I come to you humbly on behalf of the one reading this today. I pray that the spirit of God will bring peace to their mind, comfort to their heart, and hope to their spirit. I pray that healing will manifest in their life and that you will give them strength in their areas of weakness. I pray that your will bring understanding to the areas where they are confused and compassion for those that must encounter them. I pray that their family will find unity and thrive off of your love. I pray that in their pain that they find the purpose you intended for them. I thank you in advance for reviving their life in areas they thought were depleted and I pray your resurrection power and sustaining ability for them moving forward. I thank you that they have a will to live beyond their grief, pain and emptiness and are able to fully embrace wholeness and healing through Christ. In Jesus name I pray.

Troy Lee,

There was a time I thought the best gift God could ever give me was in giving you and your siblings life. I was wrong. The most beautiful gift God has given me is allowing you (to whom I gave life) to give me life again. I am forever humbled for your sacrifice of love that purpose in my life is being fulfilled.

Love,

Mama

REMEMBERING TROY LEE

I've come to the end of the road, and the sun has set for me. I want no family and friends in a gloom-filled room; why cry for my soul has been set free. You can shed tears that I am gone, or you can smile because I lived. Don't think of me as gone away; my journeys have just begun. Life holds so many facets, this Earth is but one. I am gone. Release me, let me go. I have so many things to see and do because I have loved life. I have no sorrow to die. This transcendence came with wings so that I may get lost in the blue of the sky.

ABOUT THE AUTHOR

Rose Greer is a successful, sought after businesswoman, entrepreneur, ordained minister, speaker and author. Through life-changing experiences, grief awareness, and lack thereof, Rose has become an empathetic support aide and mentor for grieving hearts and women of all ages. Rose is available for speaking engagements and workshops.

Connect with Author Rose Greer

FB: @koncreterose1004

IG: @koncrete_rose1004

www.rosegreer.com

Email: AuthorRoseGreer@gmail.com

GRIEF RESOURCES

National Suicide Prevention Lifeline
1-800-273-8255
suicidepreventionlifeline.org

National Mental Health Association
1-800-969-6642 menatlhealthamerica.net

National Alliance In Mental Illness
1-800-950-6264 nami.org

Parents of Murdered Children
1-888-818-7662 pomc.com

Zero Attempts Crisis Line
1-800-273-8255
Text SOS to 741741 (24/7 Hotline) zeroattempts.org

Disclaimer:
Please note telephone numbers may change. Hotline information/referral numbers are for reaching those who can provide crisis counseling, refer calls to local agencies and provide information and/or printed materials. We cannot guarantee the quality of services offered by the organizations listed above and no recommendation is implied.

www.ingramcontent.com/pod-product-compliance
Lightning Source LLC
Chambersburg PA
CBHW070250290326
41930CB00041B/2420